This book belongs to

____

Children's Picture/Poetry Book

I Am a Cat

by Alan Moghul

Illustrated by Marina Saumell

I Am a CaT

Published by Alan Moghul

Printed in USA

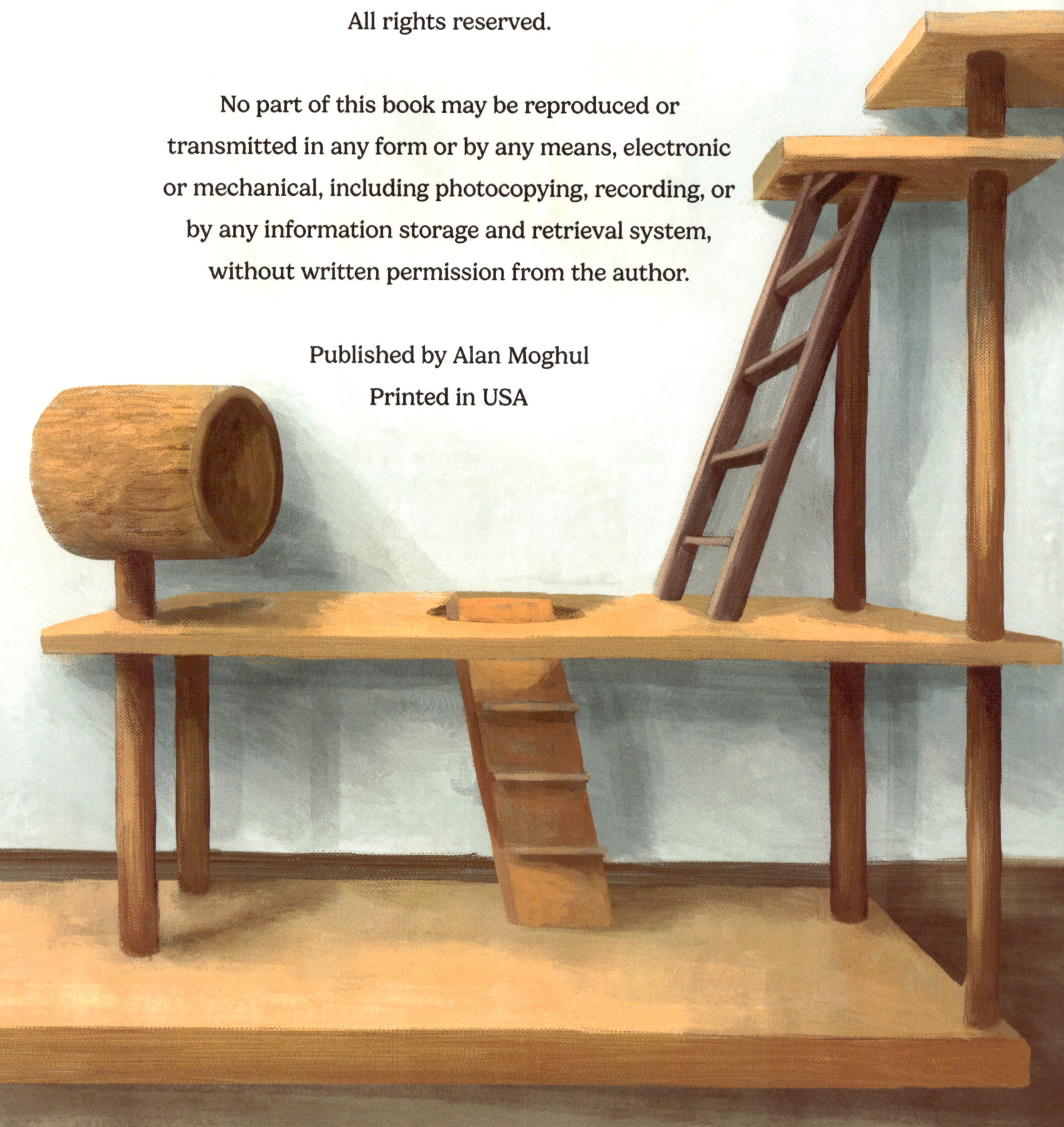

*This book is inspired by –
and dedicated to –
Alexander and Hephaestion,
two beautiful blue-point
Siamese cats who
brought us many years
of companionship,
entertainment,
and joy.*

1.

Throughout each day I give my tail a swish,

As I gaze, with longing, at my dish.

Morning, noon, and evening I have an important goal:

To see something really delicious appear in my bowl!

Throughout each day there is something on which I dwell,

For you know, I have a really terrific sense of smell.

Aside from water, having this daily is key,

And once I receive it, I immediately become filled with glee!

What am I talking about?

fer

2.

There is an activity that occupies me each day:

It involves watching eagerly every starling, wren, or jay.

I may sit near a window upon a table, ledge or chair,

My tail a-swishing, my ears erect as I stare.

For deep down I am a hunter, you should know,

This is the instinct I'm born with, and as I crouch down low,

I mimic the behavior of my relatives in the wild,

Ready to pounce and ready to run – oh my, how I am riled!

What am I looking at?

3.

Once a year my humans place me in a crate;

This is an ordeal – it's a process that I usually hate.

They take me to a place where I see animals of every size,

And a kind lady (or man) examines my mouth, my nose, and my eyes.

This person listens to my heart, feels my tummy, and looks at my tail,

And then pokes me with something that feels like a sharp nail.

Around this little room with strange instruments I'm allowed to roam,

Oh look! There's my crate – soon I will be back home.

Where am I going?

4.

Every day I like to have some fun,

Throughout the house I romp, I jump, and I run.

Whether it's a ball or toy or a feather on a string,

I perform acrobatics you might find amazing!

This activity is important – let me explain, if I may:

Pursuing a feather or toy mimics the prey

That my cousins in the wild instinctively chase;

Keep this in mind when after a ball I race.

What am I doing?

5.

There's an activity I really like when I'm not at play,

On a chair or a sunny windowsill I may lay.

I really like to curl up in my warm, soft bed –

This happens especially after I have been fed!

I lower my head, my tail is still, I close my eyes;

You know that every cat does this, no matter the size.

As with you, dear human, it's important for my body to rest,

So that – when I hang out with you – I'll be at my best!

What am I doing?

6.

Sometimes when I'm not sleeping, I'll sit on my bed,

For there's another activity I like to pursue instead.

I like to do this especially after a meal,

Please understand – cleanliness to me is a very big deal.

Using my tongue, all over my body I will lick

My face, my tail, behind the ears, even my toes I'll pick.

This routine cleans my fur and enhances the blood flow;

I might even lick another cat as a sign of affection, you know.

What am I doing?

7.

Throughout this book, dear reader, we have seen

How I like to eat, to nap, to watch the birds, and to clean

(My fur, that is); I play and sometimes must go to the vet;

All these activities show, I think it's a safe bet,

That I am part of your family, and together as we age,

We share our experiences, form memories, and go from stage to stage

Of our lives together: Human and animal bonding, this is true,

Is something quite special, for **I Am a Cat**, and I will always love you.

Answers (and additional information)

(1.) What am I talking about? **My food.**

Cats are carnivores, which means they rely on nutrients found only in animal products, such as high amounts of protein, some fat, and a few carbohydrates. Commercial cat food can be purchased as dry, semi-moist, and canned. Dry food contains between six and ten percent water and its ingredients may include meat (or meat byproducts), poultry (or poultry byproducts), grain (or grain byproducts), or fish meal. The bite-sized pieces of dry food may be coated with flavor enhancers – such as animal fat – to make it more appealing.

Semi-moist food typically contains meat or meat byproducts and is approximately 35 percent moisture. Other ingredients may include soybean meal, cereals, grain byproducts, and preservatives. Canned food has a moisture content of 75 percent, making it a good dietary source of water. Ingredients usually include meats and/or whole meat byproducts.
For further information, see
https://www.vet.cornell.edu/departments-centers-and-institutes/cornell-feline-health-center/

CANNED FOOD
DRY FOOD
SEMI-MOIST FOOD

*(2.) What am I looking at? **The birds.***

Cats – especially indoor cats – will typically spend time on a windowsill or piece of furniture looking out a window and watching birds. Cats have strong hunting instincts, and the bird is considered prey by the cat. Cats may also be intrigued by the movement, which captures their attention. Watching birds can be a pleasant and stimulating pastime for cats, and can be a good way to alleviate boredom. Other reasons cats enjoy watching birds may include curiosity, territoriality, and hunger.

Some owners observe their cats making subtle noises, such as chirping or twittering, while observing birds. This is generally believed to be excitement at seeing potential prey.

For further information, see
https://www.catological.com/reasons-cats-like-watching-birds/

*(3.) Where am I going? **The veterinarian.***

Cats should be seen by the veterinarian at least once a year. During this annual check-up, the vet performs a hands-on examination, noting the abdomen, muscle tone, fur and skin, eyes and ears, and mouth, gums and teeth, among others. Cats are very good at hiding signs of illness or pain, so it is common for the vet to take laboratory samples (such as a stool sample) to check for disease or parasites.

Always be prepared to ask your vet questions. Your vet is a trusted partner in your cat's physical and emotional wellness.

For further information, see
https://catfriendly.com/keep-your-cat-healthy/veterinary-care/

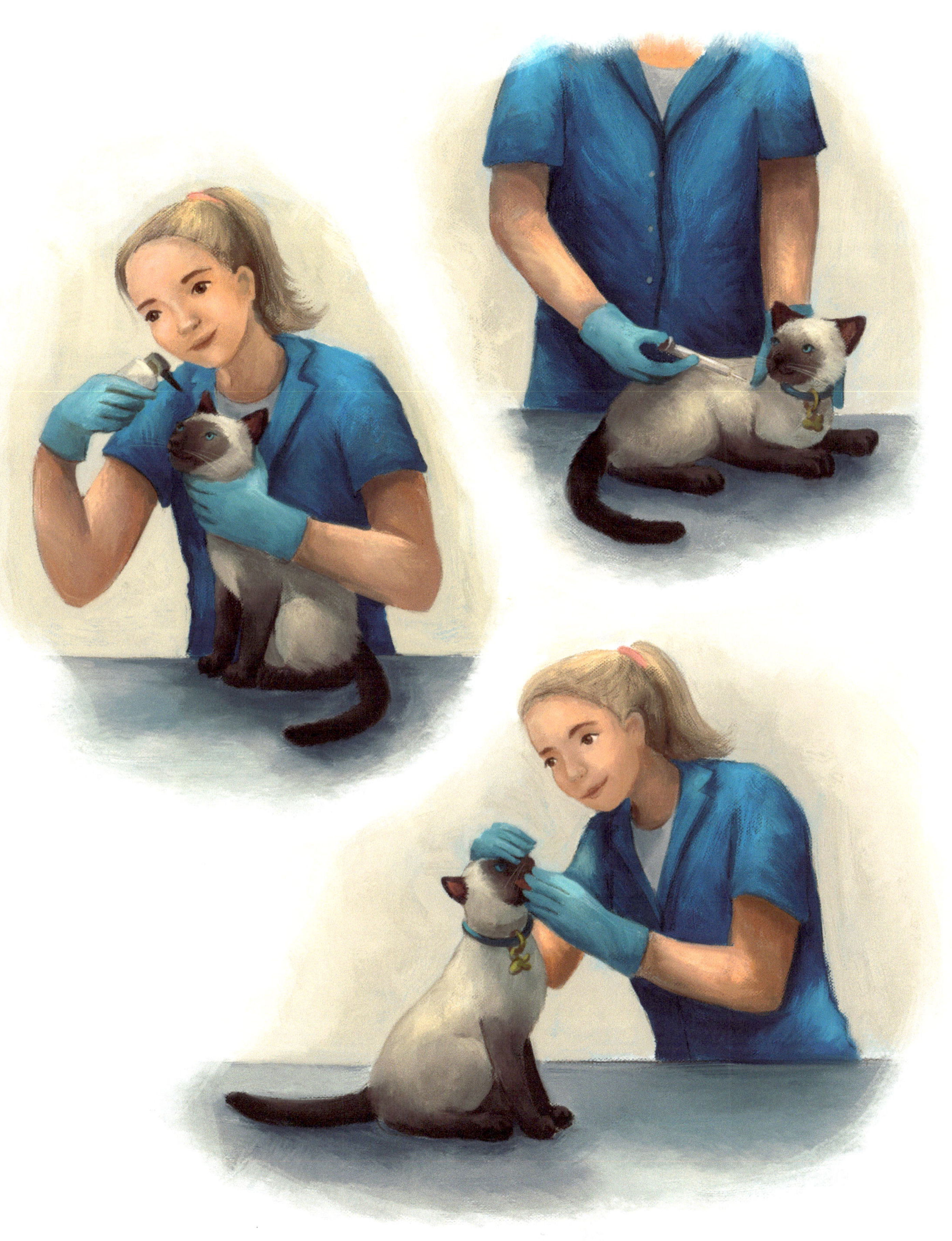

(4.) What am I doing? **Playing.**

Playing with a cat is an excellent way to let her/him dissipate excessive energy, since the play activity mimics the animal's natural hunting instinct. Play is also an important source of exercise – especially for the indoor cat – and relieves boredom for the cat.

Toys that look like small animals (mice, birds) or feathers on the end of a wand make excellent toys. Inexpensive things like wads of paper (large enough so that they can't be swallowed), cardboard boxes, or empty paper grocery bags can keep a cat occupied as well.

For further information, see
http://www.vetstreet.com/our-pet-experts/why-play-is-important-for-your-cat

(5.) What am I doing? **Napping.**

As with individual humans, individual cats will vary in their need for sleep. Typically, cats will sleep 15-20 hours each day, with newborn kittens and senior cats requiring more sleep than the mature adult cat.

It's a good idea to pay attention to your cat's typical sleeping pattern. If s/he should increase the amount s/he sleeps during the day, it could be a sign of an underlying illness, such as diabetes, kidney or liver problems, or infections. Always consult with your veterinarian if you detect a change in your cat's daily sleeping pattern.

For further information, see
https://www.petsafe.net/learn/the-truth-behind-cat-naps

(6.) What am I doing? **Grooming myself.**

Grooming is an important part of a cat's life. Grooming keeps the cat clean and helps to disperse naturally-produced oils – made by the cat's skin and fur – to keep the coat healthy and shiny. The grooming process also keeps the cat relaxed. Since cats do not sweat like humans (except through their paw pads), licking themselves keeps them cool.

In multiple-cat households, cats often groom each other, as a means of developing and strengthening their bond.

Humans can add to the cat's self-grooming regimen: brushing a cat's coat helps to remove tangles and excessive hair, which the cat ingests, potentially leading to hairballs.

For further information, see
https://www.petmd.com/cat/grooming/evr_ct_grooming